MOMENTS OF
EPIPHANY

DOUGLAS WILSON

ISBN (Paperback): 978-1-958475-25-6
ISBN (eBook): 978-1-958475-26-3

Printed in the United States of America

PROMINENT
BOOKS

5830 E 2nd St, Ste 7000 #9983
Casper, WY 82609
USA

PROLOGUE

Douglas L. Wilson grew up and has spent much of his life in the small, rural town of Grayling, Michigan. Doug is a member of the Grayling High School Alumni Hall of Fame, and he is a graduate of Central Michigan University. Doug is recently retired from a 45-year career as an educator, youth counselor, and family social worker. Doug and his wife Tracy continue to reside in the Grayling area, and they are frequent visitors of Doug's alma mater, Central Michigan University.

Wilson has been a poet for over 50 years. Moments of Epiphany is his 5th collection of poetry to be published. This book focuses on those moments of enlightenment that suddenly appear, that open our hearts and minds, and leave our lives forever changed.

Wilson reminds us of the importance of living in the moment and in living each day to the fullest. As is the case with Doug's other books, Moments of Epiphany will cause you to reflect, feel, and think.

CONTENTS

THE MOMENT OF EPIPHANY

A heavy door had swung open,
In the darkness, a lamp was lit.
At last, all of the dots connected,
And the pieces to the puzzle fit.

I could count every star in the sky.
I could smell every flower in the field.
I knew the answers to all of the questions,
And all the secrets were revealed.

All that had seemed so far away,
Had suddenly drawn near.
The mystery of life was solved,
And my path was never more clear.

For a moment, the clouds had lifted.
I caught a glimpse of that other realm.
Which lies beyond our vast horizon,
Yet to this Earth is bound.

From Heaven came a loud hallelujah,
And the birth of this epiphany.
As I enter this new frontier,
I know that God shall be with me.

2022

THE BLUE ROSE

It is winter, nature sleeps,
The sky is cloudy, winter gray,
The birds have long ago departed,
To seek a warmer place to stay.
Snow has covered the un-reaped harvest,
The orchard and its trees bend low
Covered with light frost and mist,
Gently covered in a web of snow.

All the flowers too are sleeping,
Except one rose who bends, weeping.
Boldly, she stands the winter season,
A rebel without a cause or reason.
Her petals are a bitter blue,
And frozen to the touch,
Or because she is sad, alone,
She changed her color such.
Long at last she bends her tired head,
Perhaps it only bows and prays,
But I fear inside, she's dead,
Blown by the wind she nods and sways.

Poor blue rose, sweet frozen fragrance,
Preserved in our lonely solitude,
Stretch up tall toward the sun,
Stand a century in the snow.
I have for you my empathy,
From my deepest breast.
I pray to take in and warm thee,
And put this mind to rest.
But surely God and nature will spare,
One single rose for me,
A rose of blue is very rare,
You stand alone so silently.

If only I could have your will,
To stand so tall when all alone.
Perhaps, I too could wake still,
While all the poets sleep,
Stand firm against times of grief,
Hold proud my head up high.
Tell the world of my beliefs,
And shout them to the sky.
Try to change a world found fault with,
Do those things long meant to be?
Then perhaps this anxious mind,
Could thaw its dreams in spring with thee.

1967

BURY ME (BUT NOT TOO DEEP)

The flowers wither, blow away,
Bending grass is covered over,
By wandering leaves and silent snow,
The bee has long since left its clover.

I do await that promised kiss,
Of life's last passing breath,
As passionately as I lived life,
I now shall wait for death.

Bury me, but not too deep,
In morning just at dawn,
No tears, no fears, no lament,
But hum a happy song.
From conception comes the miracle of life,
And the gift of death.

So, bury me, but no too deep,
And not within a crypt,
For I hope to feel the sunshine
Or the pattering of the rains,
Sense the landing of a snowflake.

13

Bury me face toward sky,
Where wind and clouds will pass me by,
Quietly in a patch of shade,
Where once perhaps the Indians played.

Bury me, but not too deep,
So, when winter turns to June,
A rose, might stretch and bloom,
From the remnants of my being.

Touch its dewy petals,
Feel it, and know that it's me.
Be thankful for your stay,
Here within this garden.

Blending with the lovers who made me,
From the warmth of nature's breath,
The chemicals that were beautiful,
Now inherited by this flower.

Like the unpicked fruit of autumn,
We return to our dark abode,
Replenishing what we've taken,
Our remains fertilize the globe.

So, bury me, moist deep,
Allow me to ferment.
From the earth once sent,
Must now again return.

From dust, to life, to decay,
We come, we live, and go away,
Not in darkness, nor in light,
But like the goldfinch falls from sight.

Embedded into sedimentary forms,
To lie in metamorphic silence now,
Continuing to forever mix,
With all the other elements,
Perhaps to be again unearthed,
By his children's, children's, generations.

1969

PARDON MY DUST

The clouds form and grasp the sun,
A sign to all, that day is done.
The plow has ceased its endless roam,
While weary farmers ponder home.

Noisy streets, are now but still,
The forest rings with the whipper-will.
He sings his evening rapture swell,
To the ringing of the silent bell.
Then flutters he to the apple tree,
Where the orchard meets the graveyard.

There he wails in the darkening shade,
Where the souls departed long are laid.
He echoes and bugles some final notes,
Over the dusty, silent throats,
Who, no longer merry can reply,
Nor trace his flight across the sky.

Cold and quiet they forever lay,
Wasting, withering, into decay.
Marked only by their humble stones,
Epitaphs in long and lovely poems,
Chipped of cold marble carelessly,
Inscribed upon them so poignantly.

I stop to gaze, though nature scorn,
To feel the calm before the storm.
Hidden away in the silent hush,
They are left behind to turn to dust.
Here they rest but do not sleep,
Fertilize the field but do not reap,
From their hopes, prayers, they've sown,
Across their wrinkled faces grown.

Forgotten like a wilting bloom,
Lost within the misty gloom,
Among the tall and restless pines,
They lay in crooked, humble lines.
Faces I once well knew,
Gone to quickly from my view.

They seem to lurk about the dusk,
Floating like wind about the dust,
Mixing in the feeble moonlight,
Vanishing into the dark of night,
I see the passing figures flee,
Escaped, yet caught in memory.

Not lost forever like a bloom,
But pressed upon my mind, they loom.
Unlike the patches upon my quilt,
Rather on the past, a future is built,
Not as a dove pretty, yet flown,
But as seeds of great wisdom grown.

I raised my eyes ore rippling grass,
The mind through dreams in an instant pass.
Then falls the patter of the rain,
It falls upon this lonely plain.
Falls and each droplet greets,
Forgotten faces from soft sleep.

Rain leaks upon each coffin roof,
Trampling daisies under hoof.
Wetting the cracked and humble stones,
Threatens the sky in reckless tones.
Leaves before the wind are strewn,
But all is quiet in the endless tomb.

Sudden as it starts the rain does cease,
The dampened fields are left in peace.
I leave my perch beneath my tree,
To watch the storm clouds leaving me.
Walking slowly upon my way,
I will pass by here most every day,
Wondering if when I fit my pall,
Will no one pass by here at all?
One day, I too may haunt this dusk,
And beg you, pardon my humble dust.

1969

THE GRASS GROWS GREEN

Above the glory of the storm,
Among the ever-peaceful sleeping,
Calmed, is the heart once scorned,
The wind has mourned their leaving.

Upon these ravaged hills,
Across the smoldering plains,
Weapons rust in the morning mist,
Bodies rot in the evening rains.

A terrible stench on the wind,
The vultures rose and flew,
Metals to their chests still pinned,
These children we once knew.

Here, hours ago flags were flown,
Cannons roared like heavens thunder,
Bugles echoed loudly blown,
The fields were trampled under.

The pride of every living race,
Left half-naked in the cold,
They are decomposing everyplace,
Their forms are caked in mold.

With hate and fear upon their breath,
They killed a mother's son,
Gallantly they marched to death,
Yet no one knows who won.

Twisted now in morbid shapes,
Their faces hell as seen,
Trampled like some wasted grapes,
Beneath, the grass grows green.

1969

I'M SORRY JIM

There was a chill on the wind.
The rain in a mist dampened my coat
And muddied the polish on my shoes.
The Color Guard, but faint shadows now,
Stood straight in one long row.

Pale faced, tight lipped, with red swollen eyes.
When they finally blew taps, my vision blurred,
A lump formed in my throat.
I forced a cough, for fear I'd choke.

In black your mother standing by,
Clutched the flag and wondered why,
The son she loved was asked to die,
But no one spoke, nor even tried.

Oh, Jim it could have been so good.
So long it seemed so right,
The honor and the glory,
The reason for this fight.
The New Frontier, The Great Society,
The Peace with Honor.
Where did we go wrong?

Across the Great Lakes to the north,
Some of the boys are drinking beer,
Though they must be homesick,
They are reasonably of cheer.

In Washington the message is too late,
It is now sadly clear.
There is no longer reason for us to be here.
(nor our sons in Canada either).

Oh, Jim it could have been so good.
So long it seemed so right,
The honor and the glory,
The reason for this fight.
The New Frontier, The Great Society,
The Peace with Honor?
Where did we go wrong?
What took so goddamned long?
(To learn the French lesson, the
words to Country Joe's song.)

Such a pathetic eulogy to a friend.
One who took my place.
Those that burned his flag,
The government slapped his face.
Oh, Jim it could have been so good.
So long it seemed so right.

And what of all those countless faces,
Who died in all those nameless places?
For what?
The New Frontier, The Great Society,
The Peace with Honor?
We lost!
Lost at such a terrible cost.
I'm truly sorry Jim!

For Jim 1972

SNOWBOUND IN SARASOTA

Muggy humid, almost heavy muggy.
A half-moon shines through yellowed blinds,
A restless breeze through avocado trees.
At my back door the tide is rolling in.
The screen door torn at its corners,
No longer keeps out the swarm of gnats.
Oh, the calendar lies of the season.
It goes unnoticed like so much else.
Nobody stops by anymore.
No coffee, no cards, no conversation.

The north wind is so unimportant now.
I long for the chill,
For the fragments of evergreen and snow.
The downy snow.
Whirling, twirling, sheets of white,
falling slowly, silent in the night.
The frosty art upon the windows.
Carolers singing at the door.
The merry bells ringing, icicles tinkling,
the taste of warm hot chocolate.

Oh, let the winter howl and bury!
I have forever to be snowbound.
Just give me the crackle of a fire,
The bite of an old pipe,
A hunting dog's head in my lap,
And a passing glimpse of her.
The flower I picked one spring.

Oh, this refugee with his memories!
An old fool with his pictures,
Collecting dust upon their shelves,
Alas, he amused only himself,
Lost in the heart of the south.

1973

DRAWN TO A FLAME

There is something about a candle's glow,
That comforts some, while others know.
Oh the evil behind her rays,
It radiates in such innocent ways,
To catch their eyes she gently sways.

Unknowing the valiant will vanish,
The bad, the good, all banished,
Often by their own choosing.
I have seen them come and go,
Know the buzzing of their wings,
Have felt their pain, and heard silence.

Too soon, from the fragile cocoon,
They stray, too far, beneath the moon.
Lost forever on an evening in June.
Never to go home again, unable to begin.
Drawn to the flame they singe their wings,
Alone they fall from sight,
Hardly noticed, out of mind.

The candle that is she,
Will beckon others nightly,
Shining on forever brightly,
Into the grayer hours of dawn,
Until finally, she consumes herself.
Alas, too, placed upon the shelf,
Replaced by another's radiance.

But she shall also pass,
For nothing ever seems to last,
Except the buzzing of the wings,
And the silence that follows.

1977

A LION IN WINTER

From my balcony one winter's day,
I chanced to look below,
Seeing to my amazement,
A lion in the snow.

So tired was he, so hungry,
He shivered in the cold.
Yet, stood his ground defiantly,
So stately and so bold.

He stared at me a moment,
My eyes returned his gaze.
The chill that ran through me,
I've remembered all my days.

Suddenly he gave a roar, turned,
Nowhere to go, the path left to well, marked,
Bloody paws upon the snow.
What became of this king in exile,
Of this majestic rogue?
I truly do not know.

I remember the sound of beating hooves,
The maddening cries of yelping dogs,
The muffled crackling of faraway guns,
But it happened so long ago.

Now, the vastness of these garden walls
Like that haunting memory calls,

A shadow in the twilight falls,
Like the empty echo through castle walls.

Oh, the days and deeds that were,
And the plans dared dreamed,
The trumpets blare, but a swans song,
So short lived it seems.

Marred and calloused, left trembling,
The hand that once had fed,
Bitten once too often,
To the bone alas was bled.

Then, the only music was a march,
Children all that was left to grow,
They became the harvest,
White crosses in long rows.

But I did see the robin,
I did smell the rose,
I once picked the fruit,
From the orchard down below.

The masses are at the garden gate,
And we?
Weary and somehow thinner,
As vulnerable as a lion in winter.

1980

WHAT DO YOU DO?

What do you do,
When you can't stay, nor go,
When time drifts on so terribly slow?
There is no place that you can run,
Not to, not from.
All roads lead to where you've come.

So, the heart longs, the soul cries out,
But the voice is silent in your throat.
The outside becomes as porcelain,
As the inside is now hollow.

There is no direction given,
Nor a course for you to follow.
Each new day and coming season,
Comes and goes with little reason.

So, the actor continues his mad charade,
His life an endless masquerade,
With no reprieve nor intermission,
Sinning only from his own omission.

What do you do,
When you can't stay nor go,
When time drifts on so terribly slow?
There is no place that you can run,
Not to, not from,
And all roads lead to where you've come.

1980

THE DARK SIDE

I am the dark side of me that goes on unseen.
I enter your sleep, I disrupt your dreams.
I wade in the brook, and I wander the road,
Pulling wings from the moth, and dissecting the toad.

I am the dark side of me, that smiles back at you,
For I know who you are, I know what you do.
I am the dark side of me, who is never in sight,
I vanish by day, and I sneak out each night.

I play by the well, I creep through the woods.
I have shot the sparrow, and the child if I could.
So, cry not a tear, don't utter a sound,
Just smile to yourself, when no one is around.

Because the dark side of me, is the dark side of you.
The fringe of the nightmare the world never knew.
So, come play by the well, let's
creep through the woods.
There is mischief to do, and I think you should.

For John Howard 1981

BOUNCE THE BABY

Green kites and blue balloons,
Winter nights and warm afternoons,
Pinwheels and merry-go-rounds,
Music, laughter, the quieter sounds.

The drive-in movies changing scenes,
From pink ribbons to tight-fit jeans.
Bounce the baby on your knee,
Count the fingers one, two, three.

Oh, nights of darkness, days of rain,
Stop the rocker, get my cane.
I must go out and find my toys!
I must make sense of all the noise!

The December snow is white and deep.
I am tired but cannot sleep.
Bounce the baby on your knee,
Love the child for he was me!

1983

DIRT ROADS

There is something about a dirt road,
that takes one back the winding way home,
Over miles of yesterday's memories,
to the remembrance of youth.

Oh, what a playground.
What a diary! What a canvas!
The deep centerfield.
The long and narrow grid iron.

What of the wonderous artwork, left unfinished?
Those hastily scribbled lines,
The changing initials in the valentines.

There is something about a dirt road.
The way it smells after the rain,
The butterflies fluttering about the puddles.
The flowers grace its's shoulders,
While autumn leaves trotted down,
And press against its face.

No pave them not!
For they are shaped by time.
Their age carved by the winds and weather.
Leave them to their work.
Carry the endless loads upon their backs,
While bidding good luck to the barefoot fisherman,
And take one back the winding way home.

For John Howard 1983

NIGHT'S REST

The sun fades on the whispering pines,
And the shadows start to fall.
There is watercolor in the evening sky,
And the night birds start their call.

The moonlight shall shine on fruitful vines,
And the forest looms dark and deep.
Then, a mantle of stars within the heavens,
And the world of day shall sleep.

The farmer leaves behind his plow,
|The warrior leans against his shield,
A mother snuggles her newborn son,
And the lovers inherit the field.

All that was and might well have been,
Renewed, at dawn shall start again.

1986

THE NIGHT KEEPER

It is never too far it often seems,
When horror is the night keeper of your dreams.
When evening becomes a fire fight,
And dawn brings carnage instead of light.

You live to remember that others die,
Spared by that lottery beyond the sky.
While the farm boy and the merchant's son,
Have crumpled around you one by one.
Their faces forever carved within your head,
Timelessly etched though long are dead.

There is a loneliness in a drizzling rain,
A terror when thy sky bursts forth in flame,
The burning flesh, the sounds of death,
An endless madness beneath the jungle sun,
And you the witness have seen it done.
Always wondering why you've come.

Your child shall ask, but your reply,
Shall only be an anguished sigh.
For how does one account the silent screams,
When horror is the night keeper of your dreams.

1986

THROUGH A LOOKING GLASS

The cat's in the cradle, the chalk, and the slate,
In the springtime of youth, when I couldn't wait.
With young Christopher Robin and a lady of fate,
I took my leave, through the back, garden gate.

But Alice in the looking glass, and
the man with the hoe,
Stole much of the hours, that dragged on so slow.
In quest of Merlin, I fell under his spell,
Through the gates of heaven, to the doorway of hell.

Until the green grass of summer, had turned into gold,
And the face in the mirror, had become strangely old.
For Alice in the looking glass, and
the man with the hoe,
Had disguised the events, so that I wouldn't know.

1990

THE PRECIOUS DAYS

There are fingerprints on every mirror,
There are muddy tracks across the floor.
There are toys scattered throughout the house,
Always a half-closed door.

There is a splashing in the bathtub,
There is crayon upon a wall
There is screaming in the yard,
He tends to run and fall.

There is a page missing from the newspaper
Plastic soldiers in my shoes,
A broken window in the garage,
The dog has been painted blue.

But just when you might ring his neck
He smiles and says he loves you.
He is the apple from your tree,
And there's nothing that you can do.

So fast they grow up.
Too soon they move away.
You would gladly trade the peace and quiet
For one more precious day.

For Brad 2009

CARLIE'S POEM

As morning breaks, feet hit the floor,
Cereal, pop tart, then out the door.
At her desk, a stack of books,
Heavy sighs and forlorn looks.

Math facts and a pale moon,
But May is melting into June.
A quick snack and nothing more,
A Hershey bar at half past four.

Off to see a nearby friend,
Some exploring and some pretend.
How to stop and when to start,
A bloody knee, a broken heart.

Picks through supper, chatters a lot,
What she learned and how she forgot.
Constant clutter and the reasons,
The focal point of each new season.

Half-sung songs and inside jokes,
Homemade cards and thank you notes.
Something borrowed and something old,
Her secrets shared, a story told.

A drink of water, off to bed,
A kiss on the cheek, a goodnight said.
I pause to watch, as she sleeps,
A quiet moment, mine to keep.

As I lay me down to rest,
I wonder if she has ever guessed,
How truly thankful, my heart glad,
I made the time to be her Dad.

For Carlie Jane 2010

CAST HIS ASHES

Born naked in an evening mist,
He was gently cradled and tenderly kissed.
He learned to walk, then to run,
Rocked by the tides, kissed by the sun.

He explored his world and he dreamed.
He had forever, or so it seemed.
Twas a labor of love the web he spun,
Reshaped, expanded but never done.

For the time bandit stole of his years,
It robbed him of laughter, left him with tears.
As his river rushed to the greater sea,
His dreams became but a memory.

So, bury him not within the earth,
For a future tomb raider to unearth.
No, lay him on a funeral pier,
And send him forth in smoke and fire.

Do not descend into the depths of despair,
For his very essences shall fill the air.
Allow his spirit to travel with the wind,
To distant places he has never been.

Then, cast his ashes to and fro,
To be scattered by pilgrims as they go.

2016

THE WAY

I am of the way, the truth and light.
I do not fear the dark of night.
For my shepherd takes me by the hand,
And leads me toward the promised land.

He teaches me what I need to know,
And takes me to places I would not go.
Even before my journeys cease,
He comforts me with joy and peace.

He walks with me the final mile,
And saves me from the time of trial.
Even to the very valley of death,
By still waters grants me rest.

I am of the way, the truth and light.
I do not fear the dark of night.
For my shepherd takes me by the hand,
And leads me toward the promised land.

For Paul 2016

A SAILOR'S TALE

Twas on a Saturday evening,
In a small village by the sea,
That I wandered into a tavern
A place I should not be.

The sign read "The Nautical Circus,"
An establishment most bizarre.
There was a mermaid in a glass tank,
A shrunken head floating in a jar.
A caged monkey hung from the ceiling,
And a parrot patrolled the bar.

There were whalers in long pea coats,
Tattooed pirates with their knives.
The lines upon their faces,
Told the story of their lives.
Most had sailed a lifetime,
But few had travelled far.
They kept time with the fiddle,
And one five string guitar.

I drank a tankard of rum,
And ale from a wooden keg.
I danced with a one-eyed woman,
And another with a whale-bone leg.
When alas the night was ending,
I staggered toward the door,
When I couldn't find my vessel,
I passed out on the shore.

2017

<u>I AM STILL HERE</u>

Bring on the black knight,
Your champion, your hero,
The ghosts from the attic,
The faces in the window.

I shall challenge them all,
There is nothing more to fear
My hands are now steady,
My mind is now clear.

The long winding road,
Tis at my doorway at last.
The stones within the garden,
But skeletons of my past.

From fire has come steel,
A diamond from the coal,
A pearl from the greater depths,
All fractions are now whole.

So, bring on the black knight,
Your champion, your hero,
The ghosts from the attic,
The faces in the window.

I shall challenge them all.
I have nothing more to fear.
I have danced with the devil,
And yet I am still here.

For Brock
2017

A GOLD STAR PARENT

From my window I see them come,
Up the driveway one by one.
I know the news they come to share,
My heart is broken beyond repair.

I offer them coffee and a bit of cake,
But too quickly the hour grows late.
Condolences given, they depart my door,
And I'm very much alone once more.

In the depths of my despair,
I slowly climb the winding stair.
In the vail of the darkening gloom,
I sit in the silence within his room.

There are photographs on the nightstand,
Love letters bound with a rubber band.
Upon a shelf the trophies won.
I recall the events one by one.

I ponder whether such great loss,
Was worth the gain at such a cost.
The political schemes of selfish men,
Compensate not for what might have been.

The clock in the hallway starts its chime,
But there is no point to note the time.
All the promises of his tomorrows,
Now vanished in a sea of sorrows.
All of our plans too soon undone,
To be buried with him at Arlington.

The clouds will gather in the autumn sky,
With the frost the flowers shall die,
Soon the birds will southbound fly,
And I shall forever wonder, why?

2017

A REQUIEM FOR THE DEAD

This ghastly day has ended,
In the west the sun has set,
Over these golden fields,
Where two great armies met.

The cannons no longer thunder,
The bugles no longer blow,
Gone is the roar of battle,
Fought only short hours ago.

Replaced by a somber silence,
I hear the wounded moan,
Some lay together in clusters,
While others must die alone.

The whipper wills are singing,
Their requiem for the dead.

But, what of the half written letters?
What of the songs half sung?
What of all their tomorrows,
And the work they left undone?

What of the heartbroken children,
The young wives and the lovers?
What of the tight-lipped fathers,
And their grieving mothers?

What of the friends departed,
The friends I see no more?
Even the survivors are damaged,
All casualties of war.

One day the combatants shall gather,
As if awakened from a sleep,
With joy they shall reunite,
In heaven again they shall meet.

Though overcome by sorrow,
I must soldier on.
This grim scene repeats tomorrow,
And the nights are never long.

The whipper wills are singing,
Their requiem for the dead.

I pray the birds who patrol the night,
Those angels I can't see,
When alas my time comes,
Shall also remember me.

2017

TIS NEARLY 4:00 P.M.

Tis been months since we've seen him,
Since we gazed upon his face.
We gathered for Sunday dinner,
And together we said grace.

The days have passed so slowly,
The nights so often long.
The holiday seemed so empty,
Like music with no song.

But, today he shall return,
We have well marked the date.
He shall arrive at 4:00 p.m.,
And we can hardly wait.

He has trudged through the desert,
Driven only by sheer will,
Crawled through the dirt and mud,
Crossed the rivers and climbed hills.

He has written us letters,
Only some hastily scribbled lines,
Composed between the fire fights,
When he could find the time.

He told us of his travels,
The boredom and his fear,
Of comrades that had fallen,
When the angel of death was near.

But, today we shall hear his laughter,
See that smile upon his face,
Thank the God in heaven,
For the gift of his embrace.

So, fold the morning paper,
Please hang up your phone,
Set aside your labors,
Tis nearly 4:00 p.m. –
Our soldier is coming home.

2017

A SHADOW ACROSS THE MOON

There is a disturbance in the force,
A shadow across the moon,
A tremor within the earth,
And something shall happen soon.

So long have I searched,
But the lost cannot be found.
It vanished all so quickly,
It disappeared without a sound.

It stole away the hours,
Tis like grasping at the air.
I can never quite touch it.
Yet, I know that it is there.

Scattered by a winter wind,
It is hidden in the stars.
So close, but out of reach,
So near and yet so far.

There is a disturbance in the force,
A shadow across the moon,
There is a restlessness of spirit,
And something must happen soon.

2019

<u>ECHOES AND SHADOWS</u>

'Tis late evening as I lay in bed,
The echoes and shadows manifest in my head.
Then I remember, now I can recall,
Without Ouija board or a crystal ball.

Familiar faces from out of the blue,
Every angel that I ever knew.
Some much alive, others long dead,
Every word spoken, and that left unsaid.

The events of the past, the promised tomorrow,
The bright days of triumph, the dark days of sorrow.
All of my plans, all of the schemes,
The lessons of life, all of my dreams.

A child's cries, the night bird's call,
The first sunrise, the last star to fall.
Tis nearly December, night is at end,
Only echoes and shadows on which to depend.

2018

<u>REFLECTION ON OUR ELECTION</u>

Oh, those cannibals who roam the capital halls,
they promise bridges but only build walls.
Some feed on the left, some feed on the right,
They feed each day well into the night.

They point to the debt but only spend more,
they talk of peace, yet they wage war.
Behind closed doors, they bargain and plot,
sending our finest to die and to rot.

They drive the laborers from their homes.
They tear at the flesh and gnaw on the bones.
They are not zombies, they know what they do,
They attack our churches, infiltrate our schools.

They separate the father from the mother
and pit one brother against another.
They write the rules with a thumb on the scale.
Even the free press is sadly for sale.
We are left naked and without hope.
Who can we trust? Why do we vote?

For Camren
2018

A LONG DRIVE HOME

You are perched behind the steering wheel,
A bag of peanuts for your meal.
It is not a long drive to your home,
But it can seem distant when you are alone.

Then, those flashing lights ahead,
Fill your mind with pending dread.
You strain your eyes so that you can see,
Somber faced policemen and the EMT.

A sneaker and ball glove in the street,
A crumpled form beneath a sheet.
A life now ended before it starts,
A family left with broken hearts.

You think of the teammates that he won't meet,
You picture a classroom with an empty seat.
The one true love he will never know,
All of the places he will never go.

There will be nights that you can't sleep,
A sneaker and ball glove in the street.
Every time that you shall pass by,
You will find yourself still wondering, why?

2019

EVEN TO THE ANGELS

He holds the world in the palm of his hand,
All the universe is at His command.
With a breath, He moves the clouds,
Fills the sails, and quiets the crowds.

He judges the empires great and small,
At the touch of His hand, they tumble and fall.
He has set my course over the years,
I've tended his garden, drank of his tears.

Blindly, I've wandered across the land,
When I have fallen, He's taken my hand.
Despite the gathering darkness, I have no fear,
For within my heart, I know He is near.

Even as my river is reaching its sea,
I find that He still has plans for me.
Not til the dust returns to the ground,
shall all that I've lost alas be found.

Until then, he leads, and I plod on,
Even to the angels at the gates of dawn.

To my family at St. Francis Church
2019

<u>I DON'T SEE THE LABELS</u>

They travel here from near and far,
And gather together in this little bar.
Here they will find a friendly face,
Over the years it's become their place.

Some are searching for a little cheer,
Others settle for the three-dollar beer.
Black sheep and outcasts that don't fit in,
Gamblers and dark horses that failed to win.

Artists, comics and the mischief makers,
Fallen angels and young heart breakers.
Renegades and refuges, the true rolling stone,
Condemned to wander for they have no home.

Dreamers and schemers, I've known a few,
And the best philosophers I ever knew.
Their tales of life, their stories of pain,
They waited in line, but their turn never comes.

There is more compassion than one finds in church,
You discover the soul within if you search.
Here there is some empathy shown,
Before departing for destination unknown.

So, here you may find me conversing with them,
I don't see the labels, only women and men.

2019

<u>INTO THE BLACK</u>

You can't move forward until you go back.
You must drift from the gray into the black.
Out from the light and into the dark,
Traveling to a realm that is silent and stark.

Before you measure how far you've come,
You must discover the root that you're from.
Deep into the abyss to the depths of your past,
A fleeting glimmer but it won't last.

You're trying to fill that void inside,
Trying to resurrect that which has died.
Turn into the wind and brace for the rain,
To appreciate joy you must endure pain.

Away from the light and into the night,
Reaching, stumbling as without sight,
Always searching for that lost key,
Which unlocks the door that sets you free.

You can't move ahead until you go back.
You must drift from the gray and into the black.
Exploring the recesses of your mind,
Almost afraid of what you might find.

2019

LET MY RIVER RUN

I cannot change a single thing,
For what is done is done.
So, put away your sandbags,
And let my river run.

I well recall their faces,
But lost them one by one.
I couldn't change a single thing,
So let my river run.

I have survived much heartache,
But I have also had my fun.
So, set aside your sandbags,
And let my river run.

You don't know my journey,
Nor the distance I came from.
There is no need to build a dam,
Just let my river run.

Leave me to the twilight,
Let me rest here in the sun.
Do not close the floodgates,
Just let my river run.

2019

THE GIRL UPON THE LEDGE

I found her standing on the break wall,
She was teetering upon the ledge,
Staring blankly at the ocean,
So dangerously close to the edge.

Breathing deeply with each breath,
She was blinking back her tears,
I could not know her age,
But she was young in years.

She didn't turn to look my way,
But she sensed that I was there,
Two strangers at the break wall.
With life or death to share.

I know not the cause of her sorrow,
Nor the depth of her despair,
A loved one lost, a broken heart,
So often life can seem unfair.

At last, she turned to look at me,
Her brown eyes swollen red,
On her face a look of uncertainty,
So, to the young girl I said.

"I know this hour is dark my dear,
But there will be brighter days.
You simply must believe in you,
And you shall find your way."

I stood there motionless and silent,
As the sea breeze caught her hair,
She managed to force a smile,
At the thought that someone cared.

Her body slowly began to tremble,
There was a change in plans,
She struggled to keep her balance,
So I offered her my hand.

She clamped her arms around me,
Buried her face within my chest,
She sobbed and shook uncontrollably,
Purging the fear and pain, I guess.

I gazed into the girl's eyes,
But finding no words to say,
I kissed her gently on the cheek,
And I watched her walk away.

2019

A TIME OF TRIAL HAS COME

Hold tightly to those you love,
And remember where you're from.
I can feel it in the air,
A time of change has come.

The trickle has become a river,
And no one seems to know,
Who travels with the current,
Nor where the waters flow.

The spark has become a flame,
Soon a fire out of control.
Just to survive shall depend,
On which way the winds will blow.

Hold tightly to your bibles,
Cling firmly to your guns.
You can feel it in the air,
A time of trial has come.

2020

BE A STONE IN THE FORTRESS WALL

In a world that has grown small,
You must stand up, you must stand tall.
Draw your line and refuse to flinch,
Don't concede nor give one inch.

Be a stone in the fortress wall,
Be ever ready to answer his call.
Be his sword and his shield,
You may bend but never yield.

In your heart, you know what's right,
So don't give in without a fight.
It is better to stay than it is to run,
Stand your ground until the victory is won.

You may alienate some family and friends,
But on your actions, your soul depends.
It's what you've done and failed to do,
That in the end comes back on you.

St. Francis Family, 2020

BENNY HAS A LOADED GUN

Benny has a loaded pistol,
Hidden in his chest of drawers,
I fear that he will use it,
When he can take no more.

He makes an easy target,
He's bullied each day at school.
Constantly teased and taunted,
And made to look a fool.

He hides out in the bathroom,
To escape their dirty looks.
They crumple up his homework,
And they scribble in his books.

They shove him in the hallway,
They prank him in the gym,
The humiliation is slow torture,
And no one stands with him.

But, let those bullies have their fun.
Soon the day of reckoning will come.
The hurt is boiling into a rage,
And Benny has that loaded gun.

2020

DO YOU KNOW THE PIPER?

Do you know the piper?
There are those who know him well.
He leads them from green pastures,
Into the very depths of hell.

He meets them on the corner.
He will leave them cold and numb.
Once they inject his poison,
The damage has been done.

Soon, they are compelled to follow.
In the shadows they must wait,
For once the piper casts his spell,
They find there's no escape.

Then the world grows cruel and dark.
He will rob them of their will.
Just to purchase another fix,
They will sell themselves or kill.

They follow the trail of broken dreams.
He has destroyed the plans they made.
He will suck up all of life's treasure,
Because the piper must be paid.

2020

FROM THE TRENCHES OF SOMME

They moved with an iron will,
From the trenches up the hill.
Across the fields from the mire,
Into the smoke and machine gun fire.

To protect the realm each loved so well,
They would charge the gates of hell.
With never a thought of retreat,
Those lion hearts wouldn't accept defeat.

Shoulder to shoulder, hand to hand,
Through the grass of no man's land.
A short distance now measured in hours,
Over the patches of pale white flowers.

Out in the open and less equipped,
Through the ranks the bullets ripped.
Metal through flesh and into the bone,
Many a brave lad would not reach home.

A sudden end to plans and dreams,
Farewell to family and meadow streams.
No more to work the factories and farms,
Never to lie in a loved one's arms.

Beneath the rapture of clearing skies,
For the empire they give their lives,
Leaving a trail of wounded and dead,
Stubbornly they would forge ahead.

Oh, what could persist beneath the sun,
Against long odds and heavy guns,
Steadfast until the victory is won?
Only mad dogs or an Englishman!.

2020

I TRULY WISH TO KNOW

This path seems too familiar,
Not all that far from home.
With no one to share this moment,
I'll keep this memory for my own.

I watched as the evening vanishes,
The sky has turned to grey.
There before my tired eyes,
The birth of this new day.

I stand upon this murky bank,
Of an ancient woodland stream.
I watch the fog slowly rise,
As if awakened from a dream.

The forest looms a foreboding fortress,
Balsom, cedar, tamarack, and pines.
The river bends and straightens,
On and on, and so it winds.

The dark water murmurs and ripples,
The current over the edys spill.
I am spellbound in this silence,
For a moment, time stands still.

How far has this river traveled?
How far must it yet go?
When will we reach our sea?
I truly wish to know.

2020

IF THE ROCKS COULD TALK

If the rocks could talk what might they say?
About ancient man and the world today?
What would they teach about the creation of land?
And the perfect marriage of the sea and sand?

Do they still recall that first sunrise,
When the clouds were formed within the skies?
What do they know about the passage of time,
And beyond the stars, what might we find?

Down through the ages they've existed here,
When the air was fresh and the water clear.
Before the growth of the medieval pines,
When the herds roamed free in unbroken lines.

If the rocks could talk, what might they say,
About the ascension of man and the role we play?
Do they understand both love and war,
Why it is never enough, why we want more?

As they erode in the wind and rain,
Do they experience fear, do they feel pain?
Do they grieve for what the earth has lost,
Do they believe the gain was worth the cost?

If the rocks could talk, what might they say?
About the course we're on, do they know the way?
Have they tried to warn generations gone by,
Until at last remain still, and in silence lie?

2020

MANKIND'S WAKEUP CALL?

The world doesn't seem as large,
As it seemed just days before.
Like commerce and global news,
This virus spreads from shore to shore.

Uncontained beyond the Great Wall,
The forests of bamboo,
What began in the Far East,
Has so quickly come to you.

What was once "over there,"
Is now so suddenly here.
It brings a wave of suffering,
It brings a cloud of fear.

It attacks both young and old.
It travels breath to breath.
Our healthcare is on overload,
It leaves a trail of death.

Is this mankind's wakeup call?
The cost of mistrust and hate?
What seemed vast has proven small.
Extend a hand before it's too late.

Let's set aside politics and division.
Let's make love our new religion,
Pray that out of this darkness,
Something better will have arisen.

2020

REFLECTION (AT DAWN)

The passions of the evening,
Are vanishing with first light,
The appearance of the new day,
Is quietly vanquishing the night.

The darkened sky fades to grey,
Then yellow, orange and blue.
But, I can scarcely take it in,
I have so much to do.

There is a flutter within the trees,
The songbirds start to sing,
A symphony just at dawn,
And it doesn't cost a thing.

There are droplets on the flowers,
There is a glitter upon the grass.
I try to capture this picture,
For I know this scene won't last.

Soon, there will come a bustle,
The morning doves start their coo,
So sudden gone is the silence,
And the peace that I once knew.

I find myself just hanging on,
Like a climber to the cliff.
Yet, take the time to thank the Lord,
For each new day is a gift.

2020

SEVEN MILES FROM NOWHERE

I'm seven miles from nowhere.
But, I am not afraid.
All my dreams are of the past,
There are no plans to be made.

All the truths of my yesterdays,
Are changing with the wind.
All that was of my beginning,
Is now coming to its end.

It's a long road to December.
It's been a struggle every day.
Yet, even without a compass,
I have found my way.

It's been an arduous journey.
But, I've withstood every test.
I seek the comfort of the trees,
And in their shade shall rest.

In the distance chimes the iron bell.
Might it toll for me?
I'm powerless to turn back time.
So, what will be, must be.

I'm seven miles from nowhere.
Where does one go from here?
What lies ahead is a mystery.
Yet, my course is strangely clear.

Not in the vastness of this earth,
Nor in the depths of any sea,
But, somewhere beyond the stars,
Awaits my destiny.

2020

<u>STANDING ON THE THRESHOLD</u>

You're chipping away at the ice.
You must break through the glass.
You're standing on the threshold,
Between the future and your past.

There is a perfume upon the wind.
You are waltzing with a ghost.
But, it is the next step forward,
That frightens you the most.

You've fought so many battles,
But the rules were never clear,
It's time to assess the carnage,
With that stranger in your mirror.

Your boat is drifting with the tide,
Soon it shall wash ashore,
And you are left to wonder,
What awaits beyond that door.

2020

TAKE ME TO THE LIGHT

Somewhere beyond this darkness,
There is a bright white light.
I'm ready to go there,
Won't you take me there tonight?

I'm too weary to argue,
I'm too tired to fight.
I can never go back,
Though I often wish I might.

You can take me by the hand,
Or you can swallow me whole.
I have no further plans,
And no place that I can go.

I'm surrounded by needles and tubes.
I'm hooked up to a machine.
They've pumped me so full of drugs,
That I can't even scream.

I've tried to be tough,
But this pain never ends.
I told my family I love them.
I've said goodbye to my friends.

Somewhere beyond this darkness,
There is a bright white light.
I am hoping and I am praying,
That you will take me there tonight.

2020

THE BELLS OF WARRINER HALL

You know, I find it comforting,
Although it may seem strange,
That even as I grow older,
Somethings never seem to change.

Even within the gathering darkness,
The ivy still clings to its wall,
And far off in the distance,
I hear the bells of Warriner Hall.

There upon those storied grounds,
Were the seeds of knowledge sown.
All the tools that I would need,
Once this lad had grown.

Trudging to class across the campus,
The winter winds blew cold,
But, there were late night excursions,
To Hail our Maroon and Gold.

There is a bond among the Chippewa,
You shall never feel alone,
And no matter where I've traveled,
It's there, that I call home.

Scatter my ashes at Fabiano Gardens,
Where the students passing by,
May share the peace and beauty,
Of the earth on which I lie.

I seem compelled to return each year,
Like the changing colors of fall,
And here shall I eternally remain,
Listening to the bells of Warriner Hall.

For Central Michigan University, 2020
Forever Maroon and Gold.

THE CAROUSEL

The carousel goes around and around,
The painted ponies up and down,
Never will they reach the sky,
Nor will they touch the ground.

The carousel goes around and around,
The painted ponies up and down,
Moving constant in their circle.
A calliope is the only sound.

The carnival has come to town.
But, the brass ring can't be found.
Like the plastic ponies, up and down,
Life often seems a merry-go-round.

2020

THE CLOCK IS EVER TICKING

You turn the calander's pages.
The seasons come and go.
Life has passed you by,
And you didn't even know.

The years now run together.
You find that time does fly.
There is no going back,
No matter how you try.

The clock is ever ticking,
Those hands are on the move.
You can't afford to waste a day,
Not a moment should you lose.

You've searched for the pause button,
But you find that none is there.
You know how your story ends.
It's a matter of when and where

2020

THE FATE OF TOMORROW

What is today shall surely pass,
For nothing built is meant to last.
All that is brick, mortar and stone,
The collapse of the Inca, the Persians and Rome.

The burial of Pompeii under volcanic ash,
The life of a people lost to the past.
The salting of Carthage so nothing could grow,
The death of a city that went on so slow.

The fate of tomorrow isn't so clear,
If it happened then, why not here?
You in your towers of steel and glass,
Shall fair no better in a nuclear blast.

What is today shall surely pass,
For nothing built is meant to last.
Today is a chapter, just pages to a book,
In time, no more than a glancing look.

2020

A HUMAN HEART IS A CURIOUS THING

A human heart is a curious thing,
As fragile as a songbird's wing.
It scripts the wishes that one makes,
But like the eggshell, easily breaks.

A heart seeks out what it needs,
Sorting the flower from the weeds.
A heart is true to only its voice,
And from emotion makes its choice.

A heart is given and never stolen,
It can't explain what it has chosen.
It is out of faith that the heart cares,
And only time and love repairs.

Our hearts force us to trust and try,
Brings music to laughter and tears to cry.
The human heart is a curious thing,
As fragile as a songbird's wing.

For Carlie Jane, 2020

THE LOTUS FLOWER

She is the lotus flower.
She makes the waters clear.
She blossoms in the mud,
Bringing beauty to what is near.

She asks for so little.
She takes so little care,
Just to feel the sunshine,
Just to breathe the air.

She is the lotus flower.
She thrives where others fear.
She brings both joy and comfort,
Just by her being here.

For Mary Beth, 2020

THE MIDNIGHT TRAIN

It was past time that I moved on.
So, I hopped the midnight train.
I'm sipping a pint of Southern Comfort,
Just to dull my pain.

I really need to see a doctor.
I probably should go home.
But, I'm not afraid of dying,
And I do better on my own.

Tomorrow should I wake up,
I won't remember where I've been,
A place that I've been before,
But I won't remember when.

I wander across this country,
Traveling on these iron rails,
Panhandling just to survive,
And I've spent some time in jail.

It's on the milk of human kindness,
On which my life depends.
I've met so many people,
And a couple I've called friends.

It's hard to know after all these years,
Just how far I've come.
I don't know what I'm searching for,
Nor what I'm running from.

It's from these dirty boxcars,
That I've watched the world flash by.
I believe that I could do better,
But I've grown too old to try.

I don't worry about my future,
It will work out in the end.
I feel like I've been here before.
But, I don't remember when.

2020

THE MIDNIGHT WRITER

I am the Midnight Writer,
At my desk again tonight,
Sorting the facts from fiction,
Until the dawn's first light.

I am the Midnight Writer,
I'm scribbling down the lines,
Making up the various versus,
And changing them to rhyme.

The hour has grown late,
I should be off to bed.
But, I see life in visions,
There are phantoms in my head.

I am the Midnight Writer,
Holding a comet by its tail,
Wishing upon a distant star,
But I'm not afraid to fail.

I am the Midnight Writer,
A poet with his pen,
Trying to reconcile my past,
Well aware of what has been.

If I live this life over,
I couldn't change a thing.
But, life is ever-changing,
Who knows what tomorrow brings?

2020

THE MYSTIC ISLE

There is a realm beyond our shrouds,
A mystic isle beyond the clouds.
It's beyond the equator and the polar caps,
It doesn't appear on any maps.

Should you seek this mystic isle,
The lifelong journey takes a while.
But there is an eternal treasure there,
And it awaits for us to share.

Should your ship strike a reef,
Excuse the trespasser and forgive the thief.
You must be just, you must be kind,
To every friend and stranger you find.

In time, if you find your way,
You'll find a mansion with rooms to stay.
You're never too hot and never too cold,
You never get sick nor do you grow old.

In order for you to discover this place,
You must believe, you must have faith.
But, once you reach this distant shore,
You shall live forever more.

For the St. Francis Family, 2020

TOO MUCH TONIC, LIME AND GIN

The ice is melting in the glass,
You're drowning memories from your past.
Too much tonic, lime and gin,
Causes the room to blur and spin.
The elevator goes up and down,
The whirlpool goes around and around.

You left the key within the door,
And you walk an uneven floor.
Too much tonic, lime and gin,
A warning comes from deep within.
The rollercoaster rushes up and down,
The windmill turns around and around.

Tomorrow you'll lay in bed,
A jackhammer pounding in your head.
With a mouth full of cotton,
Every cell and pore feels rotten,
And, won't you find it strange,
Once sober, that nothing's changed?

2020

TONIGHT, I FEEL LIKE MAJOR TOM

Tonight, I feel like Major Tom.
The booster is out, but the running lights are on.
All the controls had been inspected,
But this is not what they expected.

The blinking lights flash all around.
The radio static is the only sound.
There is no rescue on which to depend,
No final message that I can send.

I'm drifting farther out in space.
I find it a dark and desolate place.
I'm lost within the milky way,
Beyond the realm where angels play.

With no hope of returning home,
I am destined to die alone.
I am reconciled to this fate,
There is nothing left, except to wait.

2020

WAS IT WORTH IT?

Your world has grown rather small,
In your cell behind the wall.
Was the cost of fleeting fame,
Worth your misery and this pain?

For your violence and acts of rage,
You've been locked in this steel cage.
How does it feel to be alone,
Knowing that you'll never go home?

For the hearts you broke and the shattered dreams,
You find no shoulder on which to lean.
Where are all of your adoring fans?
What happened to your grandiose plans?

What do you see when you close your eyes,
The monster within or the dark disguise?
Who is it that you're thinking of?
Those you killed or those you loved?

Was yesterday's headlines in the news,
Worth a lifetime of paying dues?
Was being a footnote in some book,
Really worth those lives you took?

2020

BUILDING WALLS AND BURNING BRIDGES

When they could not agree,
Together they built a wall.
They built that wall real thick.
They built a wall so tall.

One side is of red brick,
The other side is blue stone.
They seem content to be apart,
And we are on our own.

Now, they're burning the bridges.
Both sides fuel the flames.
There is no crossing over,
And both sides are to blame.

The knights are walking backward,
But where are we to go?
There is no gate within the wall,
And behind us, the embers glow.

2021, dedicated to Camren Wilson

CONTENT TO COUNT THE STARS

As the daylight slips away,
I reflect upon another day.
It shall never return again,
And soon the darkness will descend.

Beneath the shadows of the pines,
I hasten to scribble down some lines.
So many things come to mind.
Yet, the words prove hard to find.

I think about my family and friends,
Of their affection and of fences to mend.
So much advice has been given,
To one who was not so driven.

I see life's treasures all around.
Within the heavens and on the ground.
Within the colors of morning skies,
And in the wonder of a child's eyes.

In the thunder of a waterfall,
In the music of a nightbird's call.
Within the murmur of woodland streams,
And in the rapture of evening's dreams.

There are those who count their money,
Constantly seeking their milk and honey.
But, I've never wished to ascend that far,
I've been content to count the stars.

2021

<u>DO NOT CRY FOR ME</u>

Do not cry for me,
Save up all of your tears,
For truly you shall need them,
As you wander through your years.

Weep for those innocent ones,
The child who was never born,
Who never lived a life,
But from the womb was torn.

Weep for the abandoned orphan,
Who is at risk for harm.
Show him your compassion,
And hold him in your arms.

Weep for those young widows,
Whose husbands perished in war.
For those who wait alone,
When boats don't reach the shore.

Weep for those who endure,
The life of the homeless man.
Try to give them some hope,
   By sharing what you can.

Weep for the political prisoner,
   Who only speaks his mind,
Punished for seeking justice,
And a world that is more kind.

But, do not cry for me!
I die at my own hand.
I freely made these choices,
And life didn't go as planned.

2021

LIVE IN YOUR MOMENTS

Nothing ever stays the same,
No matter what you do.
Life flows like a river,
And the waters will carry you.

There will be some darker days,
But hold on to your dreams.
All are eddies in the current,
Only islands in your stream.

Life's moments live as memories,
Always just beyond your hand.
Often you wish you could go back,
But alas, you never can.

Immerse yourself in every moment,
Embrace them to the last.
Live your life without regret,
For all too soon it's passed.

2021

WHAT WILL I REMEMBER?

What will I remember,
After the sadness of this day?
How family and friends had gathered,
And in silence slipped away?

The scent of the overturned earth,
The fragrance of the flowers?
The pastor's poignant eulogy,
That lasted nearly an hour?

The blue within the sky,
The melody of the birds?
The deep dark melancholy,
For which there are no words?

The etching upon the wooden coffin,
The inscription on granite stone?
The failure to choke back tears,
Or walking home alone?

What will I remember?
When there is time to think it through?
The sadness of this occasion,
Or the joy I found in you?

What will I remember?

2020

MY SPIRIT SHALL FLY

I attend church when it is empty.
I leave my fears outside.
I sit quietly in the pews,
And He sits at my side.

In the candle's light there's life.
In the darkness there is death.
I feel His hand upon my shoulder,
In my soul I sense his breath.

He raises me from the shadows,
And together we pray a while.
He forgives me for my transgressions,
He is with me at my trial.

Although my days are numbered,
I am not afraid to die.
Scatter my ashes upon the earth,
To heaven my spirit shall fly.

2021

POLLYWOGS AND FROGS

When we were young and carefree,
We would scurry down to the pond.
Two brothers with their air guns,
And we forged an invincible bond.

We would traverse the deadfalls,
And sit upon the logs.
Trace the flight of the chickadee,
And hunt the pollywogs and frogs.

We would while away the hours,
We would plot and scheme.
The possibilities seemed endless,
We lived our childhood dreams.

The years would quickly pass,
Over time so much would change,
Even the best made plans,
So often turn out strange.

We shared a common universe,
But we would live in different worlds.
He made all the money,
And I had all the girls.

I feel him still beside me,
Though he died the other night.
They say God knows what He is doing.
But to me, it don't seem right.

I am returning to the pond,
Though I must return alone.
Without him to share the memories,
I must remember them on my own.

I will traverse the deadfalls,
Sit upon those same old logs,
I'll trace the flight of a dragonfly,
And contemplate life's changes
with pollywogs and frogs.

2021, for John Boy

SILENCING THE VOICES

It's a hot and humid evening,
The night is dark and still.
He's drinking shots of bourbon,
Trying to fortify his will.

He's drifting back into the jungle,
On that trail in Vietnam.
He's walking into that ambush,
Where his nightmares first began.

Forty-five minutes in a medivac,
Six months in a hospital bed.
It was a miracle that he had survived,
But he wishes that he were dead.

He clearly sees their faces.
He still can hear their screams.
It causes his hands to trembled,
They wake him from his dreams.

All those days of therapy,
Haven't silenced these voices.
A weight is slowly crushing him,
And he's running out of choices.

His friends have long abandoned him,
And his family seem strangers now.
He has tried to escape this labyrinth,
But he has never discovered how.

He thinks about his graduation,
And the Junior Senior prom.
He recalls his high school sweetheart,
And staying with her 'til dawn.

Alone, he sits at the table,
A tortured and broken figure.
He places the Ruger to his temple,
And slowly pulls the trigger.

2021

SOMEWHERE, HE LIES ALONE

Somewhere, he lies in silence,
But no one knows just where.
If ever they should find him,
I know I will go there.

It hurts that he is not with us.
It's so difficult to understand.
He promises us he would return,
But, God had another plan.

The flags flutter above the graves,
There are flowers upon the ground.
Another Memorial Day has passed.
Yet, he has not been found.

We know that he is out there.
Somewhere, he lies alone.
One that was sadly left behind.
We need to bring him home.

For The American M.I.A. 2021

<u>TAKE WHAT YOU NEED</u>

You are looking so tired,
Overwhelmed by the fatigue.
Come rest in my arms,
Take the time that you need.

You've had a rough time,
Feel free to let go.
You don't need to tell me,
What I already know.

Cry all of your tears,
And have what is free.
There is no cost,
For this love you receive.

Take in the air,
Use me to breathe,
Take what you want,
Feel free to leave.

My body will nurture,
Use what you need.
Take a deep cut,
Don't mind that I bleed.

Come, warm yourself,
By the heat of my soul.
Stay as long as you wish.
I will heal when you go.

2021

THE ONE-WINGED ANGEL

I once met a one-winged angel,
Who could no longer fly.
I ask her what's beyond the clouds,
As I had never been that high.

Her eyes slowly begin to tear,
And she breathes a forlorn sigh.
"You must discover this for yourself,"
Came her brief reply.

I placed my arms around her.
She seemed so sad and alone.
I could not bear to leave her,
So I took the angel home.

She stayed with me for a time,
And my feelings for her grew strong.
But one morning when I awoke,
I found that she was gone.

I'm unable to get over her.
So many nights I've tried.
I've never gone beyond the clouds,
Though God knows that I've tried.

For Brock, 2020

THE WELL OF SORROWS

Near the desert village of Barrim,
You will find the Well of Sorrows,
Along the winding pilgrim's way,
And the road that they must follow.

Its age is numbered in untold years,
It's built from ancient stones,
Its belly swells with human tears,
It is garnished with sun bleached bones.

Its depth to man remains unknown.
There is grief and sadness there.
From within,
Comes wails and moans,
A crushing weight that one must bear.

They don't know what draws them here,
But in the crucifix they trust.
So, they set aside their fear,
And they kneel within the dust.

They leave the shrine without regret,
But they will remember when,
They came to cleanse their darkened souls,
And they shall not return again.

2021

ANGELS AT MIDNIGHT

The angels at midnight,
In silence drift down,
Casting their warm light,
As they gather around.

The angels at midnight,
Have descended from above,
To grant me their peace,
They still share their love.

Like phantoms from my youth,
And the spirits of today,
They have knelt beside me,
And with me, they pray.

They have forgiven my transgressions,
Though I don't know how.
Overlooking my faults,
They comfort me now.

To these angels at midnight,
So much do I owe.
What debts might I pay,
Before I must go?

Etched in my heart,
Like pressed autumn leaves,
Are those moments we shared,
All of the sweet memories.

The angels at midnight,
From the present and past,
Will faithfully keep vigil,
Until I breathe my last.

2022

GUIDE ME WITH YOUR LIGHT

Guide me with your light,
Take me by the hand.
Lead me through the dark of night,
Into the promised land.

I was lost for some time,
But I have been found.
Alas, today the dye was cast.
Scatter the ashes upon the ground.

Grant me your loving mercy,
Absolve me from my sins.
I wish to see your glory,
When my new life begins.

Guide me with your light,
Take me by the hand.
Lead me through the dark of night,
Into the promised land.

For the St. Francis Family, 2022

INSOMNIA

The Madhatter is in my bed,
And I can't fall asleep.
The sheep are roaming in my head,
And I can't find Bopeep.

My heart is in a race,
But there is no finish line.
My mind is flashing pictures,
And I'm wandering back in time.

There's white foam on the ocean,
I can hear the breaking waves.
I have entered the abandoned castle,
And explored those deserted caves.

There is a beast that stalks my forest.
There is a tide of endless sand.
All of the ghosts of the departed,
And how death affects our plans.

I've drifted into the darker realm,
The wolf is now with the sheep.
My clock is ever ticking,
But it is impossible to sleep.

2022

LET ME CROSS OVER

Walk me to that bridge,
And let me cross over,
From this forest of fear,
To your lush fields of clover.

Take me to that river,
So I might wade in,
Cleansing my soul,
And relearning to swim.

Show me the portal,
So I can step through,
Away from my past,
And to renew with you.

Lead me into battle.
Regain what was lost.
Stand fast beside me,
As I carry my cross.

Walk me to that bridge,
And I will cross over,
From this world of decay,
To your lush fields of clover.

2022, St. Francis Family

A PHOENIX SHALL RISE

The smoke is slowly rising,
From the remnants of my home.
With no one at my side,
I fought the flames alone.

My enemies have scorched the Earth,
They have poisoned every well.
They are seemingly invincible,
Even the bravest knight has fell.

But deep within the smoldering debris,
There still survives the tiny seed.
Hidden safely within the soil,
It is struggling to break free.

A dragon shall rise from the darkness,
Bursting forth from the soot.
An era of justice will soon blossom,
And the seed shall be its root.

This phoenix shall rise from the ashes,
And upward it shall fly.
Then, my enemies will scatter,
For it will patrol the sky.

2022

<u>A RED DAWN</u>

I woke up to a red dawn,
A storm was coming soon.
I climbed into my shelter,
And have stayed there well past noon.

I listen for that thunder,
The roar of the passing train.
The sound of twisting metal,
And the beating of the rain.

There is static on my radio,
The time is passing slow.
I want to escape this bunker,
But there's no place I can go.

I am sitting here in silence,
Gazing off into the space.
I am thinking of my loved ones,
I hope that they're all safe.

2022

A SUMMER STORM

There isn't any wind today,
Not a single puff of breeze,
None to stir up the dust,
Nor rustle with the leaves.

There is a calm and growing dim,
In the middle of the day.
The clouds are hanging low,
And they have turned to blueish grey.

It is a warning to leave the beach,
It is a time to go inside.
We will lie upon the couch,
As there is no place to hide.

Soon, the sky shall open up,
And the rain will ping and pound.
Soaking our entire garden,
And bending the flowers down.

But a sudden flash of lightening,
And the sound of rolling thunder,
Can't dampen our summer love,
Or break the spell we have fallen under.

Soon this angry sky will pass,
And the sun shall shine once more,
And if we are not too exhausted,
We will stroll along the shore.

2022

AN EXECUTIONER'S DAY

The cellblock is growing restless,
They're uneasy on death row.
The execution date is never posted,
Yet they always seem to know.

The coroner must pronounce them dead,
And from the chamber are lead away.
I must give a brief verbal report,
But there isn't much to say.

I'll stop at the local diner,
For black coffee and some pie.
This has become a ritual,
But I can't tell you why.

I'm making out a grocery list,
Then I'll mow the lawn.
I'll try to squeeze in family time,
Before the entire day is gone.

I'll take my children to the park,
And I'll push them on the swing.
This job has made me numb,
So I seldom feel a thing.

Execution days are much the same,
There are always things to do.
I'll throw some meat onto the grill,
And drink a bottle of beer or two.

Later on, in the evening,
As I lie awake in bed,
I'll say a little prayer,
As I erase them from my head.

Tomorrow I'll destroy his photo,
And his file must be shred,
To reach the pinnacle of my career,
All my clients must be dead.

2022

AT THE CROSS ROADS OF THE DEAD

I had suffered multiple fractures,
There were staples in my head.
I was stalled along life's highway,
At the crossroads of the dead.

Then, a spider-web of lightening,
Came bursting through my mind.
I saw her friendly face,
And hands that were rough yet kind.

She lead me to the river,
And covered me with shade.
She offered me cool water,
And some porridge she had made.

I wished to tell her of my dreams,
But she insisted that I sleep.
She softly sang a lullaby,
And I joined a flock of sheep.

I drifted about the ocean,
I wandered around in space.
I followed an amber orb,
Which returned me to this place.

They say I slept for forty days.
When I awoke the crone was gone,
But I still see her smiling face,
And hear the melody to her song.

I know that she is out there,
In the recesses of my mind.
We are destined to rendezvous,
At another date and time.

2022

BIKE NIGHT (AT THE HOLE SHOT)

It's bike night at the Hole Shot,
And they are filling the parking lots.
The event tent has been opened,
And the loud music rocks.

Harley Davidsons and some Suzukis,
Gold Wings and sleek new Spyders,
While most are piloted solo,
Some are carrying riders.

Some traveled a vast distance,
Others are from down the street.
From everywhere the strangers gather,
And soon old friends will meet.

They come to join the spectacle,
The reunion and cold beer.
With each and every new arrival,
The crowd lets out a cheer.

The rogues and the mavericks,
The riding clubs and gangs.
Those stories that they tell,
And the songs that they sang.

The faded denim and fine leather,
Bright headands and riding boots,
A tapestry of tribute tattoos,
Their gangly hair and joyous hoots.

There are rumors of some friction,
Beyond the orange retention fence.
The skulls and the crossbones,
Only add to the suspense.

But they have their own set of rules.
The unwritten code of the open road.
So, while there are moments of tension,
No bomb will explode.

By the end of this evening,
There are hugs and high fives.
It's all about their brotherhood,
And the attempt to stay alive.

You hear the roar of their engines,
See the smoke from their wheels,
You smell the heat of the asphalt,
And sense the freedom each must feel.

2022

<u>DO THESE HEROES DIE IN VAIN?</u>

Arlington sprawls as far as one can see,
Extending row by row into eternity.
Here lies our soldiers, our pilots, and sailors,
Burried with our victories and hidden with our failures.

How much blood in how many years?
So much sorrow and so many tears.
How many parents and how many wives?
How many children have given their lives?

How many jungles and how many seas?
How many deserts must there be?
If it was imperative that we stay,
How can we just walk away?

Are yesterday's plans and tomorrow's dreams,
Sacrificed for political schemes?
Do we ever know the actual cost?
Was what was gained worth such a loss?

We pause to honor these rows of stones,
As often we are able.
We carry our loved ones in our hearts,
But there are vacancies at our tables.

When they play Taps and strike our colors,
I still feel that pride and pain.
But, are we a nation of principles,
Or do these heroes die in vein?

2022

GET AWAY CLOSER

Get away closer.
Go away please!
As he comes near,
She sinks to her knees.

Her hands still tremble.
Her heart still pounds.
Her head often spins,
When he comes around.

At times, she hates him,
But she can't let go.
He has her heart,
And both of them know.

She punches his shoulder.
She pokes at his chest.
He holds her even closer,
Until she runs out of breath.

She knows that alluring look.
She is addicted to his touch.
She longs for his embrace,
And she wants him way too much.

Get away closer.
Go away please!
But she wants him to stay,
And he has no reason to leave.

2022

HIDDEN BY THE NIGHT

The enemy has surrounded me.
They are searching left and right.
I lie silently with the foliage,
Well hidden by the night.

I've never been so frightened!
Yet I strangely feel at peace.
Perhaps this nightmare will end,
And for me this war will cease.

I am not afraid of dying,
But I don't want to die alone.
I wish to hug my mother.
I'm longing to be at home.

I can almost smell the coffee,
Hear the paper boy passing by.
The neighnor is mowing his lawn,
And I can hear the baby cry.

Soon the dawn shall break.
I am praying with all my might,
That these merchants of death shall pass me by,
Before the sky gets light.

2022

IT'S ALMOST TWO A.M.

The waitress says it's 2:00 A.M.,
The bar will be closing soon.
With no reason to get up,
You'll probably sleep til noon.

You'll search until you find your truck,
And the twelve pack that you bought.
You have a ten minute drive,
If you're not killed or caught.

In the three room apartment,
That you now call your home,
You sit by the window,
And again you drink alone.

There were so many women,
That you've stopped keeping score.
You think about your ex and kids,
But you don't see them anymore.

Those so-called friends of yours,
What a pack of lousy pricks!
They would sell you into slavery,
For cheap whisky or a fix.

You tried to play the tough guy,
But you fear you're going nuts.
You've contemplated suicide,
But you don't have the guts.

You want to see the dawn break,
But the night won't let you go.
You know your life is passing quickly,
But you're dying too damn slow.

2022

MEDITATION AT DAYBREAK

In the darkness of late evening,
From this endless sea of black,
Appears the thread of golden light,
And a glimmer of hope comes back.

In the grey of the approaching morning,
Those shadows shall again appear.
But the light was lit in the distance,
And a new day is drawing near.

Those failed plans of yesterday,
Give way to last night's dream.
For a moment, all seems possible,
As those rays from Heaven stream.

The new day comes as a whiteboard,
Pure, unblemhished, and pristine.
That malais of scribbled lines,
As promised has been cleaned.

You hold the marker in your hand,
And you must create the art.
You alone shall design your future,
With each and every mark.

But there is no time to waste,
There is no going back,
The light of day passes swiftly,
And once again the sky turns black.

2022

<u>MY FOLKS DIDN'T RAISE A FOOL</u>

You tell me that you love me.
Well, I don't think that's true.
You've never shed a tear,
For all that you've put me through.

I would rather brave the jungle,
Than be locked within a zoo.
I would rather be alone,
Than spend one night with you.

I would rather join the circus,
Than be your carnival ride.
I would rather chase my shadow,
Than have you at my side.

There is an excuse or alibi,
For everything you do.
I wasn't searching for perfection,
But my folks didn't raise no fool.

To Patrick K,
2023

NOMADS AND GYPSIES

The nomads by day,
And those gypsies by night,
Rest in the shadows,
And move with the light.

Perched upon their camels,
Wagons pulled by a horse,
They seemingly will wander,
But each knows its course.

The sands of the dunes,
The grass of the fields,
Are a way from the neon,
And are far from the steal.

Their lives can't be easy,
But they remain free.
No clocks and no schedules,
No place they must be.

2022

<u>READY TO DROP ANCHOR</u>

I would gladly trade this mirror,
For a window to look through.
I am tired of staring at myself,
I'd rather gaze at you.

There's music in your laughter,
And the stars are within your eyes.
The winds are at our backs,
And the sun is in our skies.

I will happily trade the ocean,
To settle upon this land.
I am willing to drop anchor,
If you will take my hand.

I've been wandering in the surf,
Between the breakers and the shore.
But I'm putting away my compass,
I've found what I've searched for.

2022

REMEMBERING MARGARET BOWMAN

We all know Maragaret Bowman,
But no one knows her well.
They tell me that she's wealthy,
By her lifestyle, I can't tell.

She has a huge white house,
More fortress than a home.
She no longer climbs the stairs,
But wanders down stairs alone.

I know she owns a Plymouth,
But I've never seen her drive.
Her husband was her chauffeur,
But he's no longer alive.

She ventures out on to Pensylvania,
Turns right on Ottawa street,
Wollen coat, a red knit hat,
And rubber boots upon her feet.

She has never owned a cane.
There is no one at her side.
She will not seek assistance,
And she won't accept a ride.

The sidewalks have grown treacherous,
She shakes her salt upon the ice.
Her steps have become unsteady,
And I hear she's fallen twice.

It's only a one block journey,
But it takes longer than you'd think.
She's walked this vast distance,
In order to purchase her cranberry drink.

She never buys any groceries,
Nothing she might eat.
No bread, no milk, no canned goods,
Not a single slice of meat.

She will leave two bills upon the counter,
She never waits for change.
She often mutters to herself,
And the children find her strange.

She will not take her purchase home,
But will leave it at a neigbor's door.
It's her way to feel connected,
And each day she buys more.

She will return again tomorrow,
If she can survive the night.
They she lives on borrow time,
And I suspect they might be right.

2022

SEARCHING FOR THE EXIT

Your tomorrows are in your past.
You are running out of time.
You are searching for an exit,
But it's proving hard to find.

You're remembering with a sigh,
That your well is almost dry.
There is no way to go back,
And yet you often try.

Your entire life is on replay,
You're existing on "Come what may."
There's a sudden urge to speak,
But what is left to say?

All your days have faded grey,
You wish to go but you must stay.
Your world is growing silent,
And nightly alone you pray.

Oh, if only you could fly.
With the angels way up high.
But this is not your day to die,
And you laugh so you don't cry.

Your life has nearly passed,
Lost to the sands of time.
You're looking for your exit,
And it's proving hard to find.

2022

SHE GIVES ME BUTTERFLIES

She gives me butterflies,
So I bring her flowers.
She makes me laugh.
We often talk for hours,

There is a dinner and a movie,
And she holds my hands.
She's entering my dreams,
She's changing my plans.

She's that rare summer silence,
That unexpected winter thunder.
I can't awaken from this dream,
Or the spell that I am under.

Every moment is like poetry.
There is an enchantment to her touch.
I would give her the moon and stars,
But she never asks for much.

Each night, I wish and pray,
I'll get down upon one knee,
And give her all of my tomorrows,
If she'll spend her life with me.

2022

SILENCING A LONE REED

Countless arrows fill my sky,
Shot from untold bows.
Why I'd become their target,
I'm not certain that I know.

I don't disrespect my fellow man,
I don't persecute a soul.
But I refuse to join their herd,
And follow where they go.

I am but a single reed,
Blown in a restless wind.
Longing for a distant past,
That shall never come again.

But should I scale the mountain,
They would surely push me down.
Should I tempt to swim upstream,
I'm afraid that I would drowned.

The arrows will return to earth,
I've known this from the start.
I can't escape the coming torrent,
And some will find their mark.

Then, far off in the distance,
You will hear those archers cheer.
They will claim their victory,
And the sky above shall clear.

2022

THANK YOU AND GOODBYE

I've come to say "I'm sorry,"
But I'm not so sure just why.
I'm not looking for a fight,
And I don't wish to make you cry.

There is a restlessness about me.
There's a shadow across my path.
All the promises of yesterday,
Have faded with the past.

I know that you still love me,
And God knows that I try.
But it's time to open the bastille door,
And the let this caged bird fly.

The sun will shine within the sky,
The breeze will ripple throught the grass.
The river shall rush to its sea,
But not everything will last.

One day, I might look around,
And find myself alone.
But no matter what roads I travel,
Not one will lead me home.

I'm here to say "I'm sorry,"
Though I'm not sure just why.
I'm struggling to find some words,
To say thank you and goodbye.

THAT FORK IN THE PATH

During a recent glimpse of my past,
I could clearly see that fork in the path.
But I was too young to know,
Which way I was supposed to go.

One fork was trampled nearly flat,
Easily followed without a map.
The other path was in need of wear,
And I sensed a dark foreboding there.

I avoided the path of Robert Frost.
I never stumbled nor got lost.
I settled for a life of compromise,
Traded blue skies for little white lies.

Oh, what a hand I might now hold,
If only I had been told,
When it was safe to gamble,
And when it was best to fold.

Should I have taken the riskier way?
I find this difficult to say.
But I've learned one painful fact,
Once you choose, you can't go back.

2022

THE BACK ABBEY ROAD

The back abbey road,
Winds down to the moore,
Where once a great ocean,
Has receded from shore.

The gathering of the night mist,
Becomes a dense fog.
It dampens one's cloak,
And turns footpath to bog.

With no stars to guide you,
One is easily lost.
But those that might hunt you,
Can be easily crossed.

The moan of the scottish wind,
Is the only sound you hear.
But even in the darkness,
You can feel that she is near.

Here, often would they meet.
He would kiss away her tears,
While they plotted their escape.
And set aside their fears.

But on that very night,
That they had planned to flee,
She strangely failed to show.
Wherever might she be?

What might have kept her?
Has something gone terribly wrong?
All alone in the darkness,
He would wait til it was dawn.

She had disappeared from home,
Vanished without a trace.
Gone too was her diary,
And her white gown with lace.

What became of his love,
Remains a sinister mystery.
Perhaps foul play or black magic,
It remains unrecorded history.

His heart was left broken,
His spirit was shattered.
He could never move forward,
She was all that had mattered.

Some promises must be kept,
Some bonds cannot be undone.
A life that has been planned by two,
Cannot be lived by one.

The back abbey road,
Winds down to the moore,
Where once a great ocean,
Has receded from shore.

The moan of the wind,
Is all that you hear,
But alone he still waits,
For his lost love to appear.

2022

THE SNOW ANGEL

The downey flakes fall silently,
And land in her flowing hair.
Her winter coat is partly open,
But she doesn't seem to care.

She has that rare angelic beauty,
Her dark eyes like ambers glow.
Her red shows and matching hat,
Are cast upon the gathering snow.

She wears a single strand of pearls,
She cradles a bouquet of flowers,
Which I suspect were a gift,
As those shops don't keep late hours.

She pauses beneath the street lamp,
I see her breath in the cold night air.
I wish that I was an artist,
So might capture the aura there.

As she passes by,
She smiles.
But she doesn't speak a word.
She sound of my beating heart,
Is all that can be heard.

She vanishes into the shadows,
Walking quietly alone.
The streets are all but deserted, I
pray she makes it safely home.

THEY SHARE THE SAME WELL

Abraham was the founding father,
The elder of his tribe.
He gathered together a vast flock,
And God was at his side.

Protected by Immanual's promise,
And the coming of that star,
He would build a great nation,
Right here where we are.

But what of Ishmeal the outcast,
The banished brother and son,
The black sheep of the desert,
And the battles that he's won?

Mohammad, the great prophet,
Has risen from the sand,
A warrior and a teacher,
His people claimed this land.

So, who is the more righteous?
This is difficult to tell.
They must breathe in the same air,
And they drink from the same well.

2022

TRIBUTE TO A FALLEN HERO

I have sought him in the shadows,
In the valley of the dead,
Through the smoke and fire,
Where the creek with blood runs red.

Once he soared with eagles,
He slept within the lion's layer.
Even in those darkest hours,
He was always there.

He has charged the cannonade,
He has never known retreat.
He could always keep his head,
In the midst of a battle's heat.

But where has he gone?
In some shallow, unmarked grave,
Returned once more to the Earth,
From the life he freely gave.

There will be no monument,
No mourners to wale and weep.
But I shall whisper a prayer for him,
Tonight before I sleep.

2022

<u>WORLD OF DARKNESS</u>

It's a terrible place to live,
It's a lousy way to die.
I wish to run away,
But I'm too weak to try.

While I was sleeping,
Something went terribly wrong.
This is night is never ending,
There is no coming dawn.

I want to see the sun,
I want to feel the rain.
But I'm exiled to this place,
Condemned to endure this pain.

This is a world of darkness,
Not a star within the sky,
I want to light a candle,
But I'm afraid to try.

What has happened to my courage?
What has happened to my dreams?
Frozen within this icy sphere,
And dormant so it seems.

2022

A SIMPLE POETS LAST REQUEST

I do not want to be a leaky faucet,
Which drips drip by drip,
Turning the white porcelain a rusty brown.

I wish to be like a light switch,
Which can be easily and quickly shut off,
So that the room gets suddenly dark.

I do not seek out a headline nor tribute,
I wish to fade away like an afternoon fades.
Fading into nightfall.

Let my last day pass quickly by and without fanfare.
Just bid me farewell,
Cover the face of my clock,
And commend my spirit to the eternal yesterday.

2023

AROUND AND AROUND

Around and around,
Hand within hand,
We followed the circle,
To where we began.

Sometimes we go up,
Sometimes we down.
We move to the music,
Which has no sound.

Around and around,
Hand within hand,
The circle has lead us,
To where we now stand.

Take one step forward,
And then a step back,
We are seeking a treasure,
Without any map.

Around and around,
Hand within hand,
We follow the circle,
Without any plan.

Always your first,
And always your last,
We move in our circle,
Til our time has passed.

Around and around,
Hand in hand,
We follow the circle,
To where we began.

2023

<u>BLACK DUCKS</u>

Just beyond this meandering river,
There is a pathway into the cut,
That leads you through the marsh,
To the sanctuary of the black duck.

It's not yet daybreak,
But I know this trail well.
I've slipped and I've stumbled,
But I've never fell.

Through the long green grass,
Through the mud and black muck,
One must be determined,
When you seek the black duck.

I can smell the scent of balsom,
See the first rays in the sky.
The fog is slowly rising,
And falling leaves catch my eye.

Down closer to the water,
At the edge of the pond,
They gather in flocks,
Flying above and beyond.

You don't need your dog,
A watch or your phone,
You don't take a friend,
You hunt black ducks alone.

What is left to capture?
I have no desire to kill.
I have this moment to myself,
I wish to freeze it still.

The scene flows across the canvas,
Each brush stroke made with care.
Appearing and then disappearing,
As warm breath in the air.

You immerse yourself in the silence,
Drape yourself in peace.
All that has encumbered you,
Will slowly be released.

I think back to my youth,
I remember old hunting friends,
How swiftly does the time pass,
How quickly does life end.

But some things never change,
The seasons come and go.
The leaves will color and fall,
The winter winds will blow.

I hear a distant passing plane,
The freeways, cars and trucks.
But I'm hidden safely here,
Among this flock of ducks.

2023

BURNING THE SHIT HOUSE DOWN

Some folks call us shady,
Vengeful and plain crazy.
And there isn't a soul in town,
That doesn't believe we burned the shit house down.

Ben Boggs was a nasty old man,
Cold hearted, vulgar and mean.
He had a terrible temper,
The likes that few have seen.

He often insulted our mothers,
And would make us children cry.
You could never seem to avoid him,
No matter what you might try.

He would push and push,
Until he would cross the line.
There would be retribution,
That was only a matter of time.

So, when he shot our dog,
Right there on the spot,
Me and Harley vowed our revenge,
And we hatched an evil plot.

Stick matches from a kitchen drawer,
Some coal oil from the mill.
All wrapped up in a bandana,
And hid out at the still.

When Boggs ran out of supplies,
And he headed out for town,
We brothers snuck through the woods,
When no one was around.

The privy door was wide open,
There was nothing you might lock.
So, we tossed in our fuel,
Into that nasty box.

We crept a little closer,
But when I dropped the match,
There was a flash explosion,
That knocked us on our ass.

The shit house was engulfed in flames,
What happened was hard to tell,
But we got up off the ground,
And both of us ran like hell.

They saw the smoke in Spotsville,
And they did the best they could.
But when they struggled up the hill,
All they found was the smoldering wood.

They blamed a kerosine lamp,
Probably left on over night.
But Boggs weren't no fool,
He knew this wasn't right.

The next day me and Harley,
Sat on grandma's porch.
Both our hair had been singed,
And our eyebrows had been scorched.

Neither of us uttered a word,
We never did confess.
Of all the stunts we ever pulled,
This was easily our best.

I don't regret what we did,
Not even for a minute.
I only wish that old son of a bitch,
Had been sitting in it.

2023

EVERY ROCK IS UNIQUE

You are standing in the men's room,
There's graffiti on the wall.
There are cartoons and lines of poetry,
Etched upon every stall.

Brief messages and names,
With numbers you might call.
Written by the desperate and the lonely,
And those about to fall.

You watched the inner-city artists,
Create their box car art.
Some will paint the masterpiece,
All will leave their mark.

There are masters within the group,
But you don't know their names.
Yet their art is well displayed,
As it tours on passing trains.

You walk down any urban sidewalk,
And find the street musicians there,
Beneath the canopies on ever corner,
You will find them everywhere.

They're an undiscovered treasure,
They play, they sing, they dance.
There's a magic in their music,
That holds you in a trance.

So few will shine like diamonds,
Most of us are stones.
We will build the walls and bridges,
And communicate with phones.

But every rock is unique,
Each has a story to tell.
If you wrote them into a book,
I'm quite certain they would sell.

2023

I SHALL WALK A DIFFERENT PATH

The sunlight filters through the trees,
Exposing the dust upon their stones.
Often they will lay in clusters,
But most will lie alone.

Hidden away in the ghostly silence,
Buried deep within the ground,
They long to hear a familiar voice,
But they cannot hear a sound.

The world that they once traveled,
Is now condensed into one spot.
All that they have ever learned,
Is contained within this plot.

I shall walk a different path.
So burn my body into ash.
Hide me into flowers,
Let me melt into the grass.

I wish to hear the scurrying crowd,
And watch them as they pass.
Time moves like a river,
And the current is swift and fast.

The blue eyes and the brown eyes,
Every color and every creed,
Are searching for what they want,
And finding what they need.

Welcome to the Fabiano Garden,
It's a little peaceful park.
A quiet place for the morning students,
And the lovers after dark.

Here they will find their poet,
Scattered about the grass.
Faithfully keeping his vigil,
A relic from the past.

Oh the history I have seen.
All the stories I could tell.
Beside the splashing fountain,
And beneath the tolling bell.

The memories are well preserved,
With the secrets of the past.
Poetry bound into books,
In hopes that they might last.

2023

IS THE SKY ABOUT TO FALL

In my canyon, I heard an echo,
It came from my distant past.
We once promised our tomorrows,
But sadly, it wouldn't last.

There were puddles along the roadway,
A wave blew through the grain.
There were droplets upon the leaves,
Left over from the rain.

There must be a portal,
That takes one back in time.
There must have been a glitch,
That froze you in my mind.

If God might grant me wings,
Would I have the courage to fly?
Am I am ember in your darkness?
Or a meteor in your sky?

In my canyon, I heard an echo.
It was your anxious call.
But am I the oasis in your desert,
Or is the sky about to fall?

2023

MY ROCK AND MY SAFE HARBOR

When you hold me in your arms,
You take away my fear.
You infuse me with your courage,
Even as danger nears.

When you hold me in your arms,
You soothe away life's pain.
You have become my shelter,
That shields me from the rain.

Everyday is another battle,
Some come casting stones,
Some will tear your flesh,
Others will break your bones.

So often tired and wounded,
I have struggled through your door,
And you remain my shield,
Protecting me from this war.

Your arms are my safe harbor.
You saved me from the storm.
You have never asked of me,
You have kept me safe and warm.

In this world of dark illusion,
I have found what is real.
But how might I thank you,
Or express the love I feel?

2023

ONE LAST MOUNTAIN

There is one more river to cross.
I can see the other side.
I am searching for a crossing,
And the Lord shall be my guide.

I have crossed the burning desert,
Through a swirling sea of sand.
I was nearly blinded,
But he took me by my hand.

There is one last mountain to climb.
I am summoning all of my will.
He shall meet me at the summit,
And my heart with joy shall fill.

I will enter that promised pasture,
So peaceful, vast and green.
All of His flock will gather there,
To share in the eternal dream.

2023

<u>ONLY AFTER A RAIN</u>

After a summer storm,
The meadow brooks will flow.
Once the leaves have changed,
The water fowl will go.

From the grayest of days,
Comes the freshest of snow.
Only after the long winter,
Will warm breezes blow.

Only after the spring rain,
Will the wildflowers grow.
Only from our pain,
Follows the joy that we will know.

Only after night's darkness,
Is borne the new dawn,
And the plainest of the birds,
Often sing the best song.

2023

ONLY TIME WILL TELL

Our joy follows our sorrows,
As day will chase the night.
At the end of every tunnel,
You will find a ray of light.

What drives us to our knees,
And leaves us awake in bed,
Will vanish like a morning fog,
And turn our night skies red.

No mountain will be too high,
No sea will be too vast,
No desert will be too dry,
And the winter will not last.

Our destinies lie here before us,
But there's a bottom to every well.
What lies beyond our horizon,
Only time will tell.

2023

RELIEF AT THE LAKE

I put the work week behind me,
And I'm heading to the beach.
I can almost hear those lapping waves,
And feel the calming peace.

The winters are cold and long,
But I return each June.
Tell the gulls and loons,
I will be with them soon.

The sun is slowly sinking.
There are diamonds on the water.
I think I left my computer on,
But right now it hardly matters.

I'll watch the lights of the fishing boats,
Blue Gill, Perch, and Bass.
I used to live to fish,
But that's mostly in my past.

I shut off my cellphone.
I've opened the tanqueray.
I'll grill myself a steak,
And put away this day.

I'll get up early tomorrow,
And have coffee on the beach.
The fluffy clouds and summer breeze,
Shall bring me much relief.

2023

RISKS AT COSTA BUENA

Costa Buena is a beautiful place,
A blue sea with sun bleached sand,
Tiki bars and endless space.
It is truly a remarkable land.

She came down from up north.
She's a long way from home.
Down here for spring break,
And she has come alone.

She's the classic Barbie,
Just looking for some fun.
She is spread out on her blanket,
And she is soaking up the sun.

But there are hidden dangers here,
There are rules to understand.
There are bull sharks in the shallows,
And land sharks prowl the land.

She must study the fins,
Know a porpus from a shark.
She should not swim alone,
And never after dark.

A land shark has no fins,
In schools they stalk the beach.
Hidden beyond their raybans,
Always a cooler within their reach.

Flip-flopped and bare chested,
They seek a night of fame.
They can tear a heart apart,
Until little of it remains.

Soon, she hears their cat calls.
They get up into her face.
Is this the attention that she sought?
I hope she packed her mace.

Costa Buena is a beautiful place,
A blue sea and sunbleached sand.
But if you choose to visit there,
There are risks you must understand.

2023

SHE

She has quietly entered into my soul,
And caused the pounding in my heart.
She's the lighthouse amidst the storm,
And the lamplight in the dark.

I can feel the warmth of her body,
I know her gentle touch.
At times I can barely breathe,
I love this girl so much.

I don't know what tomorrow brings,
Nor what arrives upon the tide.
But I know that I am a better man,
When she is at my side.

For Tracy
2023

TAKE ME HOME TO DIXIE

I'm seated at the table,
With a steel-eyed river boat gambler.
A former confederate gunrunner,
And a Yankee carpet bagger.

I've had a good run of luck,
But I'll celebrate alone.
I can hear the banjo music,
And I'm longing to go home.

Take me home to Dixie,
Down the flowing Mississippi,
Where the magnolias are in bloom,
And moss is hanging from the trees.

Take me to the land,
Where the bayous and mountains meet.
Lead me through the quiet orchards,
And down the bustling streets.

Show me those great white mansions,
And the never ending fields.
Down those red clay roads,
To those Sunday chicken meals.

Place a belle within my arms,
With eyes of Bonnie blue.
The lady with those southern charms,
And a bit of devil too.

Take me to the land of Bobby Lee,
Down this mighty Mississippi,
Where the cotton grows high,
In the home that I call Dixie.

The drums of war are silent now,
The battle flags are put away.
But the stars and bars forever wave,
Over her sovereign grave.

2023

THE EMOTIONS WE FEEL

She is to my night,
What I am to her day.
At the birth of the dawn,
Together do we lay.

Immersed in our fantasy,
Which has become just as real,
As those moments that we share,
And these emotions that we feel.

When we are spent,
And we lapse into dreams,
Like dew upon the meadow,
Or the mist upon the stream.

Even without wings,
We shall upwardly fly,
And play within the clouds,
At the end of the sky.

We are as constant,
As the moon and the stars,
The rings around saturn,
And the red sands of mars.

The love that we share,
These emotions we feel,
Are as a gentle as a kiss,
Yet tempered like steel.

When we have awakened,
And lie breath to breath,
We vow our commitments,
Beyond even death.

2023

THE LAUGHING COW

Once there was a laughing cow,
Which lived on Meadow Lane.
Each morning it went to pasture,
At evening we turned home again,

It would walk the fence line,
And watch the children play.
On those hot summer days,
It stayed within the shade.

When I would approach her,
A curious event took place.
She would puff out her cheeks,
And a smile would cross her face.

Then I could hear her chuckle,
Soon a full blown laugh.
It would make me giggle,
And it helped the long days pass.

Then she would shake her head,
And turn and walk away.
But I could see the spectacle,
Nearly everyday.

Sometimes it's lonely on the farm,
And she became my friend.
My life was ever-changing,
But on her I could depend.

I never knew why the bovine laughed,
I don't know what happened to that cow.
As I grew up we moved away,
And we lost touch somehow.

2023

THE PUPPET MASTER

Our lives are not our own,
And our futures remain unknown.
There is a master in control,
And only our destiny does he know.

Last night's cryptic dreams,
Like a hot coffee steams,
Rising slowly from our cup,
They disappear as they rise up.

Our plans lie tangled upon the floor,
And we can't exit the open door.
Our ship has left the shore,
Unable to return once more.

There is a master in control,
And he decides where we shall go.
Our world is shaped by ancient hands,
And we move at his command.

Our lives are not our own,
And our future remains unknown.
The master controls every string,
Causing us to dance and a caged bird to sing,
With a tug upon each string.

2023

THE SKELETONS IN YOUR CLOSET

The skeletons within your closet,
Are armaments in their chest.
You've tried to hide your past,
But they won't let it rest,

All the lies and secrets told,
Are now headlines in the news.
The game is coming to its end,
And you're about to lose.

The verdict has been given,
But for the sentence you must wait.
You don't need a crystal ball,
You already know your fate.

All of your dirty laundry,
Is hanging out on the line.
There's kinks within your armor,
Have eroded over time.

Your apologies and condolences,
Alas have come too late,
And the ghosts of your victims,
Are gathering at your gate.

2023

THE STRANGERS ON A TRAIN

They have never met,
Just two strangers on a train.
Yet they feel a connection,
As their lives were much the same.

Neither one was married,
But each one had a home.
Both of them still searching,
As they often felt alone.

She had a quiet beauty,
And he couldn't help but stare.
She had those warm adoring eyes,
And that long dark flowing hair.

Being with her was comfortable,
No need to pretend nor lie.
He could simply be himself,
And his fantasies could fly.

She had waited for so long,
There had been disappointment and pain.
Was the one she had longed for,
Now beside her on this train?

Everytime she looked at him,
Her heart would skip a beat.
Not for money, nor for gold,
Would she exchange this seat.

He had that manly rugged look,
But an easy going style.
He was charming and attractive,
With a warm and engaging smile.

He might listen when she speaks,
He might hold her in his arms.
He could keep her safe,
And protect her from life's harms.

They became lost in conversation,
Giving more than they took,
She was the angel of his dreams,
He was the hero in her book.

They had never met,
Just two strangers on a train.
But from the moment they sat down,
Their lives wouldn't be the same.

Both have missed their destinations,
But neither seems to mind.
They will travel hand in hand,
Til the last stop on the line.

2023

THEY ARE NO LONGER FREE

Once the buffalo grazed these meadows,
But an owl has perched in the tree.
Once the people roamed these prairies,
But they are no longer free.

They saw the clouds within the sky,
They must have smelled the rain.
The world was lush a beautiful,
Before the white man came.

All they wished was to be left alone,
But we would not let them be.
There was a battle at the Little Big Horn,
And the massacre of Wounded Knee.

Going on their painted ponies,
Like the feathers from their hair,
So many promises have been broken,
And the treaties so unfair.

Some nights you can still hear them,
Around their fires they chant.
They often dream of going back,
But alas they know they can't.

The snow is melting from the mountains,
But the owl remains in the tree.
Once the people roamed the prairies,
But they're no longer free.

For Tony
2023

<u>UPON A PORCELAIN PONY</u>

I used to sleep around,
So that I would not get lonely.
It was a patch of rough road,
Upon a porcelain pony.

Every night was an adventure,
It was a life of danger.
I slept with one eye open,
And would wake up with a stranger.

I drank my share of alcohol,
And stayed out until the dawn.
There were plans and promises,
But something would go wrong.

But as I grew older,
I would settle down.
Happiness could not be bought,
In a bar or club in town.

I'm eating meatloaf and apple pie.
My life has changed so fast.
I'm sleeping with the cook,
Trying to escape my past.

Now I'm happy to be at home,
When here I am never lonely.
But it's been a rough ride,
Upon a porcelain pony.

2023

<u>WHEN EVERY DAY IS TUESDAY</u>

When every day is Tuesday,
Unchanging and overcast,
You're longing to move forward,
But you're shackled to your past.

You feel lost within a crowd,
But no one is around.
You wished that you could rise,
But you're tethered to the ground.

The doctors that attend you,
Can't interpret what you've said.
They don't share the visions,
Nor hear the voices in your head.

When every month is March,
And your world is covered in snow,
You want to escape the monsters,
But there's nowhere you can go.

For Brock and Carlie
2023

WHILE YOU WERE DREAMING

Last night, while you were dreaming,
I gazed upon your face.
I took a mental snapshot,
That time will not erase.

It is only a simple photo,
For me alone to keep.
A moment in the moonlight,
As I watched you sleep.

There's no need to cast you in plaster,
Or to encase you in cement.
You haven't changed at all,
Since the first time that we met.

No artist at his easel,
With canvas in colored oils,
Can capture your natural beauty,
No matter how long he toils.

It's not a masterpiece at the louver,
Nor a portrait one might find.
It's just a mental snapshot,
In the gallery of my mind.

2023

<u>WHAT I'VE COME TO KNOW</u>

It's a long and winding road,
With every twist and turn.
Life is filled with lessons,
You should take the time to learn.

Not everything you need to know,
Is taught while you are in school.
You must live with a purpose,
And practice the golden rule.

It's easier to wage a war,
When it's not your child you send.
When you manage another's wealth,
It's much easier to spend.

It's easier to greet someone,
Than it is to say goodbye.
It's often harder to tell the truth,
Than it is to flat-out lie.

Sometimes you must let go of,
The one that you love the most.
It's going through a life together,
That makes a couple close.

It's easier to run down hill,
Than it is for you to climb.
It's difficult to know the future,
And impossible to turn back time.

Money has a limited value.
Your treasure is family and friends.
They are the ones you lean on,
When the road comes to its end.

For my friends and family
2021

<u>ACKNOWLEDGEMENTS</u>

Moments of Epiphany proved to be a challenge for me to write. The genre tends to be somewhat darker and more philosophical than my other four books. There is a fine line between getting the reader to feel and think, versus depressing a reader. Finding the correct track proved somewhat difficult. A series of health issues, financial concerns, and a change of publishers, caused a delay in the completion of this book. Thank you all for your patience.

My sincere thanks goes out to my family, friends, and fans who continue to support and encourage my writing. A special thanks goes out to my daughter Carlie Jane, who's typing, editing, and artwork were a huge factor in the completion of this book.

<u>NOTES</u>

If you've enjoyed Moments of Epiphany, you may
wish to read Echoes and Shadows, Into the Black,
Well of Sorrows, and Angels at Midnight. All four
of these collections of poetry may be purchased
through Amazon, Walmart, and Barnes & Noble.